To my wife Tracy, for being my partner in ministry and for providing the inspiration behind the tools that we believe will make the church healthy again.

To Kenzie and AJ, our kids who make parenting easy with their teachable hearts and a desire to become the disciples Jesus envisioned all along.

To Scott, Gerrod, Steve, Ross, Dave, Chris, Tom, John, Eric, Carl, Shawn, Joel and the entire staff at Alpine Church for putting up with one crazy idea after another.

To Steve, Joey, Paulo, Joseph, Miko and others at Victory for keeping church simple and modeling the one thing we should have been doing all along.

To JD, Chad, Mike, Doug, Cory, Alex, Pat, Sean... and to everyone who joins the movement to help people pursue God around the world.

Prologue

On September 9, 2001 we held our first public worship service at Alpine Church in Utah. Two days later the twin towers fell in New York City, and the world would never be the same. For our church, though, the real life-changing moment wouldn't come for another decade.

This book is about our ministry and the lessons we learned after an unexpected and inspiring visit the Philippines in 2009. It's about how we discovered that even though we thought we were healthy, we soon discovered that we weren't the church Jesus envisioned. We were broken, and my guess is that your church is broken too.

I'm not writing this book to criticize or point fingers. I'm writing it because I love the church, and we've finally learned how to fix it. The solution is simple and certain and a little bit boring. I saw the fix at work in Victory Church in Manila, and we're beginning to see it applied at our church in Utah.

"Slow is fast," they told us on our first visit. We believe it, and we're committed to seeing it through.

This book is for anyone who cares about the church: pastors, elders, small group leaders, and everyday Christians. But more than anything, it's for my two kids. I want them to know what it looks like to be the church Jesus envisioned. And I pray that they will see the impact of that kind of church in their generation.

Ch 1. One Thing Makes a Church Great

"Pop quiz!" blurted Pastor Jun Escosar, director of the School of Missions for Victory Church in the Philippines. He had seen us slip into the back of the room.

Pastor Jun continued. "You hit the ground in a closed country, and you don't know a soul. You have nothing but the clothes on your back. What is the first thing you do?"

My mind raced. I was a competitive student, and I was certain I knew the answer. After finishing a graduate degree from Wheaton, my wife Tracy and I had moved to Utah to plant a church. We had lived this pop quiz, and we survived to tell the story. Alpine Church was the fastest growing Christian church in Utah at the time, and in my heart I was proud.

Back to the question. "Get a job," I thought to myself. After all, that's what I did to supplement our small missionary support. I had my contingency answers lined up as well. "Write a good sermon," "Produce a great church service," "Get the right staff on the bus." These were all backup answers, and I was certain one of them was right.

Pastor Jun called on a young Filipino in the third row.

"Make one disciple," he answered.

Pastor Jun smiled. "That's right. Just make one disciple. That's how you start a healthy church."

The Ephesians 4 Church

There's only one thing that makes a church healthy and future-proof, and without it the church is dead already. It trumps buildings and location and staff, and it has nothing to do with how much money is in the bank. It's the secret sauce of the early church and it's the key feature of the faith community that Jesus envisioned for every generation. It's glaringly missing in most American churches today and yet it's unbelievably easy to fix. The singular purpose of this book is to help you get the vision for this one thing and to empower you to become a part of the solution in your home town, whether you're a pastor or just an average joe Christian.

The one thing every church needs is disciple-makers.

A disciple-maker is someone who steps up and looks outward and helps people pursue God. He or she lives on purpose and answers the call of Jesus in the Great Commission, given 2000 years ago to his original disciples. A disciple-maker realizes that the greatest thing a person can do in this life is to help someone pursue God, and the second greatest thing a person can do is to help *someone else* pursue God.

A church full of disciple-makers is the church that Jesus envisioned.[1]

Ephesians chapter 4 paints this picture for us. Paul describes how a healthy church functions with such simple clarity that it is a wonder the church ever lost its way.

> ***Ephesians 4:11-12*** *Now these are the gifts Christ gave to the church: the apostles, the prophets, the evangelists, and the pastors and teachers. Their responsibility is to equip God's*

---

[1] https://www.pursuegodnetwork.org/the-great-commission-and-your-ministry/

people to do his work and build up the church, the body of Christ.

Read those verses again. Did you catch what Paul is saying? These verses are about strategy. Like a great coach, Paul is handing out the job descriptions for everyone in the church. He's teaching that if the pastors and the people would just understand and play their role, it would revolutionize the church and the world.

Verse 11 starts with the ministry leaders - in today's terms the pastors and paid staff members at church. Their job is to equip and empower the people to do the work of the ministry, to help the people be disciple-makers. Pastors are not just supposed to preach better sermons and put on nice events. They are tasked with mobilizing the people who are following Jesus to go out and help others follow Jesus.

The pastors equip. The people make disciples.[2]

Is this what your church looks like? If not, you're broken.

When Google first entered the online playing field in 1996, it was nothing compared to the mega business of Yahoo. Yahoo was the search engine of choice. Do you remember how it worked? It was a destination website. If you wanted to find information on the internet, you would visit Yahoo.com. It was the mega portal, the great keeper of information (and of paid advertisements). And to get our business, it had a massive marketing budget to attract visitors. Remember the commercials? Yahooooo!

---

[2] http://www.pursuegod.org/why-make-disciples/

Google had a different idea. Instead of creating a destination, it created a service. Instead of forcing users to come through its portal site, it distributed itself throughout the web. Its strategy was to freely embed itself everywhere, opening and gifting its code to the world. While Yahoo was forcing the world to come to it, Google was going out, bringing their product into the world.

And that strategy paid off in the end. By 2013, Google had literally decimated its competition, with a market capitalization 10 times higher than Yahoo. In that same year, Google reported revenues of 59 billion, compared to just 4.6 billion for Yahoo.

While Yahoo was spending millions in marketing and trying to draw customers to its site, Google was quietly and freely embedding itself everywhere on the web. Google exploded with its viral method, and Yahoo tanked with its outdated strategy.

Google, not Yahoo, is a model for the church Jesus envisioned.

The Diaspora

When Jesus gave his 40-day seminar to his disciples after his resurrection, Jerusalem was the hub of Christian activity on the earth. Whatever followers Jesus had were gathered in that city, awaiting instructions from their resurrected leader. He didn't disappoint, casting a larger-than-life vision.

> ***Acts 1:8*** *"But you will receive power when the Holy Spirit comes upon you. And you will be my witnesses, telling people about me everywhere—in Jerusalem, throughout Judea, in Samaria, and to the ends of the earth."*

After speaking these inspiring words, Jesus ascended into heaven. The disciples stood there confused, staring into heaven without a clue. Two angels suddenly appeared beside them and spoke.

> **Acts 1:11** *"Men of Galilee," they said, "why are you standing here staring into heaven? Jesus has been taken from you into heaven, but someday he will return from heaven in the same way you saw him go!"*

Jesus had done his thing, and now it was time for the disciples to do theirs. "Quit standing around," quipped the angels. "Get to work." And so they did. The book of Acts records the mind-blowing growth of the young church, from a small band of average people to a massive movement that would change the world.

But the early church didn't have the resources that our churches have today - TV, radio, podcasts, websites, Bible colleges, seminary-trained pastors, or the Bible answer man. They were a ragtag bunch of followers, without capital or buildings or the internet to spread their message. The result was a deep dependence upon the Holy Spirit and the all-in participation of regular Christians. In the early church, disciple-making was a thing. If you were a follower of Jesus, you were in the business of making disciples.

But the movement threatened the established religious hierarchy of Judaism. Persecution came, and Stephen was killed by a Jewish mob in Acts 7, becoming the first Christian martyr in history. That event seemed to open the floodgates.

> **Acts 8:1** *A great wave of persecution began that day, sweeping over the church in Jerusalem; and all the believers except the*

apostles were scattered through the regions of Judea and Samaria.

The great persecution threatened to quell the momentum of the early Christian movement. The believers were scattered abroad, separated from their beloved apostles. They had no Bibles. They had no pastors or organizational structure. The establishment leaders must have sensed victory.

But what the Enemy meant for evil, God used for good. The believers went out from Jerusalem and started making disciples wherever they landed. Like Google, they embedded themselves in their culture. The great persecution catalyzed the missional church that Jesus envisioned in the opening chapter of Acts. It's worth looking at again:

> ***Acts 1:8*** *"But you will receive power when the Holy Spirit comes upon you. And you will be my witnesses, telling people about me everywhere—in Jerusalem, throughout Judea, in Samaria, and to the ends of the earth."*

What Jesus predicted in Acts 1:8 became a reality in Acts 8:1. The disciples - all of the believers, not just the apostolic leaders - became witnesses for Jesus, first in Jerusalem and then in Judea and Samaria, and soon enough to the ends of the earth. It was a church where the people were equipped by the apostles and empowered by the Spirit to do the ministry of disciple-making.

Just like Jesus envisioned.

Can you imagine what might have happened if the great persecution hadn't taken place? If today's church is any indication, the answer seems obvious. The people would have gotten comfortable. The church would have stagnated. A culture would have grown up where the apostles did the real ministry and the people did the consuming. The church would have bought buildings and become an institution, and the sense of mission and purpose would have died in the hearts of average believers. Peter and John would have become celebrity preachers, and everyone would have invited their friends to come listen.

It would have looked like our churches today.

But by God's grace, persecution broke out against the church - and the truth of the gospel was forced into distribution mode. Rather than being concentrated at the top and guarded by massive institutional structures, the task of disciple-making was released to the regular people. This was the intentional strategy of Jesus himself. He wanted to work in and through ordinary people. From the get-go, people were his plan.

A Bunch of Yahoos

Today, the success of institutional Christianity has broken the church. We have lost sight of what brought victory to both the early church and Google. Rather than distributing the truth and embedding ourselves in the world, we have forced people to come to us. In an age where Google dominates, we're acting like a bunch of Yahoos.

And it has gotten worse. When people don't come (and they are not coming), we satisfy ourselves with sitting back and cloistering among our Christian friends. We have forgotten our singular mission, the one thing we are supposed to do well. Instead of going out into all the world to be a witness, we stay in our safe Jerusalems.

Meanwhile, Satan is using the Google strategy. He doesn't operate buildings and institutions. He has simply embedded himself into every home and school and business in our society. He is getting his message out loud and clear, advancing his mission that runs counter to ours.

His goal is to keep people from pursuing God. And he is winning.

Jesus never wanted the concept of the church to be mistaken for a building or an institutional hierarchy. The church is a people, committed as a community to bringing the message of Jesus to the dying world that so desperately needs it. Jesus envisioned a church that was embedded in the world, one Christian at a time.[3]

---

[3] http://www.pursuegod.org/heres-the-real-reason-no-one-makes-disciples/

Ch 2. The Strategy Is in the Long Tail

Blockbuster long dominated the movie rental industry, capitalizing on the big hits as their name suggests. Their business model was built on the mass market appeal of the most popular movies, and those movies raked in the bucks.

Then Netflix showed up.

Netflix took a different approach. Instead of depending on the few big hits to keep their business afloat, they offered a much wider variety of content. Without the ball and chain of brick-and-mortar stores, Netflix had the freedom to expand into smaller niche markets. They found success in the strategy of the "long tail".

Imagine a graph that represents profits from a company's products. The handful of top-selling products are on the left side of the distribution curve, representing a healthy profit margin because of the high number of sales. That's called the "head". On the right side of the curve is the tail, the large number of products that have much lower sales totals. In a traditional business, the tail is often dead weight that represents products that might need to be eliminated. But in the case of Netflix, the long tail was the key to its success.

Rather than relying on the income of the head - a few blockbuster movies that carried sales for the rest of the library - Netflix could afford to diversify into the mass niche market, offering everything to everyone through its simple organization and efficient distribution method. As a result, they made money on the long tail as well as on the head - while their competitor was dependent on just the blockbuster sales. Netflix had a business model that would dominate the digital future.

But Blockbuster never saw it coming. In 2000 they passed on purchasing the fledgling Netflix for $50 million. By the end of the decade Netflix would have 20 million subscribers and over $2 billion in revenue - while Blockbuster would be filing for bankruptcy.

The First Followers

According to the Bible, a healthy "Ephesians 4 church" is one where the pastors equip and empower the people to go make disciples. But this idea didn't originate with the Apostle Paul. It was actually Jesus' idea, and we see it in action at the start of his ministry.

The first followers of Jesus were not the highly educated, socially positioned, or religiously sophisticated elite of his day. Jesus could have picked anyone for the important task of building his church, but he chose average people.

> ***Matthew 4:18-20*** *One day as Jesus was walking along the shore of the Sea of Galilee, he saw two brothers—Simon, also called Peter, and Andrew—throwing a net into the water, for they fished for a living. Jesus called out to them, "Come, follow me, and I will show you how to fish for people!" And they left their nets at once and followed him.*

The fishermen were regular guys, just going about their ordinary business. They weren't looking to make a career move. They were not celebrities and had no illusions of changing the world. But Jesus called to them, and they responded. They went all in, and they would soon start a revolution.

Jesus was a master strategist, and he modeled how to grow a movement. He intentionally poured into a handful of average guys, and then he equipped them and sent them out to do just what he did, empowered by the Holy Spirit.

> ***Matthew 28:18-20*** *Jesus came and told his disciples, "I have been given all authority in heaven and on earth. Therefore, go and make disciples of all the nations, baptizing them in the name of the Father and the Son and the Holy Spirit. Teach these new disciples to obey all the commands I have given you. And be sure of this: I am with you always, even to the end of the age."*

After training his disciples, dying on a cross, and raising from the dead, Jesus gave his followers this singular task, the Great Commission. Then he left.

That's it. That was his vision. Disciple a handful of average guys. Then empower them to do the same thing.

The Fisherman Dilemma

Think about the dilemma Jesus must have faced. These fishermen were the working class of Jesus' day. They had little experience in reading the scriptures. And what about their lack of clout in society? Would anyone even take them seriously? In spite of the obvious downsides of choosing these regular guys, Jesus called them to follow him. And somehow - in the proximate future that Jesus had accurately envisioned - the church would explode under their ministry.

What possibly could have qualified these fishermen for the massive responsibility ahead of them? The Jewish religious leaders of the day were the first ones to stumble upon the answer.

> ***Acts 4:13*** *The members of the council were amazed when they saw the boldness of Peter and John, for they could see that they were ordinary men with no special training in the Scriptures. They also recognized them as men who had been with Jesus.*

They had been with Jesus. That was their only qualification. They had no institution-approved training or badges of honor. They were not experts in the law and they had no religious pedigree. They were simply discipled by a carpenter's son who had been rejected by the establishment. And when their leader left, they too were rejected by the religious elite. But they pressed on with the mission, standing firm in the task Jesus had called them to.

> ***Acts 4:18-20*** *So they called the apostles back in and commanded them never again to speak or teach in the name of Jesus. But Peter and John replied, "Do you think God wants us to obey you rather than him? We cannot stop telling about everything we have seen and heard."*

Peter and John had the courage to stand up for God's truth in the face of an established religious institution. The religious leaders tried to bully and intimidate them. But they had a higher authority, and with that came a very clear message and mission. Like the prophet Jeremiah, their calling was a fire shut up in their bones. They had to get the message out, no matter who objected.

In today's culture we've sidestepped the fisherman dilemma with our Christian professionals. Seminary has trained up our pastors to share biblical truth in an increasingly complex society. The natural result is to leave the task of disciple-making to our own trained professionals, the "Blockbusters" of the church. The average Christian doesn't feel qualified or commissioned to do ministry, and the result is obvious. With just a handful of pastors doing top-down ministry, the massive "tail" of the church - millions of average Christians around the world - remains anemic and inert.

Nick was a quiet, unassuming man from a southern province of the Philippines. He had been attending our church in Utah for several months, but I first met him in preparation for a missions trip to Mexico. Little did I know that Nick was a powerful, influential businessman with great vision and an impressive skill set in computer programming. But his influence on me would have nothing to do with his work life. He was the one to introduce me to Victory Church.

At the time, Victory Church was a massive multi-site church with over 35,000 attenders in campuses throughout metro Manila. Nick had come to faith through the church in his college years, when Victory was still in its early stages. I learned about it when Nick and I spent a week together in Mexico. As we drove to our worksite every day, Nick tried to convince me that Alpine Church was just like his church back home. I couldn't understand how our tiny church in Utah could be similar to a massive church in Southeast Asia, but Nick insisted that it was true. The more he talked, the more intrigued I became. This church was bigger than any church in the US. Why hadn't I heard of it? And what could we possibly share in common? It sounded like a stretch.

Nick offered to take me there so I could meet the leadership team. Within months I was on the plane with Nick and Steve, a co-pastor at Alpine who would investigate this mysterious church with me. When we landed in Manila, we had no idea what a dramatic impact this church would have on our ministry back in Utah.

Steve and I were given backstage access to Victory's top leaders, and we were quickly impressed. With 13 campuses and over 70 services every weekend, Victory Church had live teaching at every venue. Many of those venues were city shopping malls, one of which we visited on the weekend. When we got to the mall, we worked our way through a massive crowd waiting outside the door, held out by security guards at the entrance. The previous service was just finishing up, and it had to clear out before the next group could come in. Soon we were all scrambling to find seats and the walls quickly filled up three rows deep with a standing-room-only crowd. The music and teaching was great, but to our surprise, nobody acted like a rock star. In fact, because of the multitude of quality leaders and communicators, we had no idea who was in charge. It was exciting and confusing. We had never seen anything like it.

In our experience, megachurches in America had a clear formula: rock star teacher + rock star band = lots of spectators. But at Victory Church, either everyone was a rock star or no one was. And we couldn't tell.

And it turned out that nobody was really just a spectator after all. We started talking to the attenders to try to discover Victory's secret sauce. Why were all of these people coming? The answer surprised us. It wasn't about the exciting services after all. Every person we interviewed was there because of a friend, not because of a rock star celebrity. Ordinary relationships with regular people had brought them in.

Victory was the kind of church that Jesus envisioned.

Beyond Celebrity

For the 3 years of Jesus' ministry on earth, no one could draw crowds like he could. He healed the sick, walked on water, miraculously fed thousands, and even challenged the arrogant religious elite. People wanted to see this, and they traveled for miles to get a glimpse. Jesus was an all star.

> ***John 6:1-2*** *After this, Jesus crossed over to the far side of the Sea of Galilee, also known as the Sea of Tiberias. A huge crowd kept following him wherever he went, because they saw his miraculous signs as he healed the sick.*

In today's church a celebrity like Jesus would be a gold mine. We would put him on stage whenever possible. We would maximize his platform and get him his own weekly TV spot. We'd make t-shirts, coffee mugs and bumper stickers to expand his personal brand. We would market the celebrity of this great miracle worker and communicator, and we would do it all to the glory of God.

But Jesus took a different approach.

> ***John 6:3*** *Then Jesus climbed a hill and sat down with his disciples around him.*

Even as the crowds pressed in, Jesus broke away to be with his small group. He had a different strategy than our celebrity-driven churches today. Instead of maximizing his personal platform and doing the blockbuster work himself, he was satisfied with pouring into the fishermen he was equipping. And soon enough he released them to do the work as well.

> ***Luke 9:1-2*** *One day Jesus called together his twelve disciples and gave them power and authority to cast out all demons and*

> *to heal all diseases. Then he sent them out to tell everyone about the Kingdom of God and to heal the sick.*

Jesus knew he could draw bigger crowds on his own, but he resisted the temptation to do the work himself. He took a longer view of the task, and he empowered his followers to carry the message into the world.

And in the next chapter he sent out an even larger group of disciples.

> ***Luke 10:1-2*** *The Lord now chose seventy-two other disciples and sent them ahead in pairs to all the towns and places he planned to visit. These were his instructions to them: "The harvest is great, but the workers are few. So pray to the Lord who is in charge of the harvest; ask him to send more workers into his fields."*

Jesus sent 84 followers to go make disciples, and his biggest prayer request was for more workers. Jesus understood the strategy of the long tail.

> *"Tell us a little about your faith journey." I was standing outside Victory Church in Manila, and I grabbed the first guy I could find. I want to see how universal their discipleship culture really was.*
>
> *"I came to faith at Victory two years ago," he said. "Miko discipled me."*
>
> *"Wow. That's great. Who's Miko?"*

"Oh, he's an old friend from college. He discipled me, and now I'm discipling three of our other friends. Two of them are getting baptized this month. It's exciting to see what God is doing at Victory."

This was what almost every conversation sounded like during that week in Manila. Everyone used the same word. Without prompting, people would naturally start talking about "discipleship". Everyone was discipled, and everyone was discipling. I was confused.

"What exactly do you mean when you say Miko discipled you?"

Blank stare. I kept digging.

"Is that a thing here? Is there a system or a process?"

Again, hesitation. The answer seemed obvious to him, and he was shocked by my ignorance. He knew I was a pastor, and that made him even more confused.

"Discipleship is relationship. Miko knows me, so he just invited me to go through the 'One to One' booklet. I turned him down for a long time, but eventually I was ready. He talked through the booklet with me and helped me to see my need for Jesus. After I accepted Christ, he invited me to Victory and I went through the next steps, getting established and equipped in the Christian faith."

It seemed so natural. I was amazed at the clarity that this guy had.

"So when did you start discipling others?" I asked.

"Right away. I started praying about who to engage in my life, and a few friends came to mind. So I brought them through 'One to One'. I did the same thing for them that Miko did for me."

"Wow." I didn't have any other words for it. But he had one more thing to add.

"And soon they'll do the same thing with their friends."

Pentecost

Just after his ascension, Jesus illustrated his commitment to the long tail strategy in dramatic fashion. After promising to empower his followers to be disciple-makers in Acts 1, Jesus poured out the Holy Spirit in the next chapter to equip them for the task.

> ***Acts 2:1-4*** *On the day of Pentecost all the believers were meeting together in one place. Suddenly, there was a sound from heaven like the roaring of a mighty windstorm, and it filled the house where they were sitting. Then, what looked like flames or tongues of fire appeared and settled on each of them. And everyone present was filled with the Holy Spirit and began speaking in other languages, as the Holy Spirit gave them this ability.*

The disciples never saw this coming, and they must have looked at each other in confusion as this strange event unfolded. Why all the different languages? The answer soon became obvious. It was the strategy of the long tail.

> ***Acts 2:5-11*** *At that time there were devout Jews from every nation living in Jerusalem. When they heard the loud noise,*

everyone came running, and they were bewildered to hear their own languages being spoken by the believers. They were completely amazed. "How can this be?" they exclaimed. "These people are all from Galilee, and yet we hear them speaking in our own native languages! Here we are—Parthians, Medes, Elamites, people from Mesopotamia, Judea, Cappadocia, Pontus, the province of Asia, Phrygia, Pamphylia, Egypt, and the areas of Libya around Cyrene, visitors from Rome (both Jews and converts to Judaism), Cretans, and Arabs. And we all hear these people speaking in our own languages about the wonderful things God has done!"

Regular people from every nation were gathered in Jerusalem for the festival of Pentecost, and Jesus seized upon the opportunity. Just as he had chosen fishermen three years earlier through whom to spread his message, now he was choosing these faithful and average Jews in the Pentecost crowd to carry the message back to their homelands. They all heard the praises of God in their native tongues, and then Peter preached his first sermon in their common dialect. Thousands came to saving faith in Jesus, and the disciple-making strategy of Jesus carried forward.

Soon they would all be back in their homelands, without a pastor or a church but empowered nonetheless to spread the message they had heard in Jerusalem. Jesus didn't send celebrity preachers into Mesopotamia, Judea, Cappadocia, Pontus, Asia, Phrygia, Pamphylia, Egypt, Libya or Rome. He saved regular people on the day of Pentecost, and then he sent them.

Later in the book of Acts we find Paul and Barnabas travelling on a missionary journey to share the good news of Jesus with the Gentiles. Once again a blockbuster disaster was narrowly averted.

> ***Acts 14:8-12*** *While they were at Lystra, Paul and Barnabas came upon a man with crippled feet. He had been that way from birth, so he had never walked. He was sitting and listening as Paul preached. Looking straight at him, Paul realized he had faith to be healed. So Paul called to him in a loud voice, "Stand up!" And the man jumped to his feet and started walking. When the crowd saw what Paul had done, they shouted in their local dialect, "These men are gods in human form!" They decided that Barnabas was the Greek god Zeus and that Paul was Hermes, since he was the chief speaker.*

Paul and Barnabas could have basked in the afterglow of their god-like status, but instead they used their platform to point the people to Jesus. Returning later to Lystra, they appointed leaders from among the people and invested in the long tail.

> ***Acts 14:23*** *Paul and Barnabas also appointed elders in every church. With prayer and fasting, they turned the elders over to the care of the Lord, in whom they had put their trust.*

This passage serves as a great illustration for the church today. We elevate our celebrity pastors to a place of honor, electing them as chief speakers as they preach in our church buildings. But Jesus would rather have *regular people* carry the message to the world, not just the preachers.

Jesus, Paul, and the early strategists of the church worked hard to steer the people away from a blockbuster mentality. The message of the gospel would be brought into the world by average believers everywhere, not by a handful of celebrity leaders. This is the church Jesus started with his first disciples, and it's the church he still envisions today.

The spring before we planted our church in Utah, I took a trip back to my hometown of Naperville, Illinois. I visited the church where my wife and I were married and where I launched my first youth group. In the hallway between services, the senior pastor saw me and flagged me down. I told him that I was preparing to plant the church in the fall, so he offered to connect me with a renowned church consultant who was a faithful member at the church.

Just hours later I was sitting in the consultant's living room having tea and talking church-planting strategy. I had no money and few connections, so I took advantage of this serendipitous opportunity. I took copious notes.

"So what's your plan?" he asked, wisdom in his tone.

"Well, I think we'll be multi-site and team-led. I want a space that fits 200 to 300 people, big enough to create energy but small enough to feel like everyone matters. We'll go from one service to two services to three, and then we'll split off into another campus."

I had charts and floorplans. I mapped it all out.

"Here's the main thing," he said, cutting to the chase. "Whatever you do, preach good sermons. That's your job. It all starts with good sermons. Make the service attractive, and you'll attract people. That's how you'll grow."

He was right, and we did grow. But it didn't grow the church that Jesus envisioned.

The Pharisee Complex

The Pharisees were the religious elite of Jesus' day, but they had a superiority complex. They relished the gap between their high place of honor and the lowly level of the commoner. To add to their hypocrisy, they studied the scriptures but failed to apply them. They articulated the letter of the law, but they missed God's heart behind it. Jesus scorned the Pharisees for their arrogant attitude. They were the bad guys of the New Testament.

> ***Matthew 23:1-7, 11-12*** *Then Jesus said to the crowds and to his disciples, "The teachers of religious law and the Pharisees are the official interpreters of the law of Moses. So practice and obey whatever they tell you, but don't follow their example. For they don't practice what they teach. They crush people with unbearable religious demands and never lift a finger to ease the burden. Everything they do is for show. On their arms they wear extra wide prayer boxes with Scripture verses inside, and they wear robes with extra long tassels. And they love to sit at the head table at banquets and in the seats of honor in the synagogues. They love to receive respectful greetings as they walk in the marketplaces, and to be called 'Rabbi....' The greatest among you must be a servant. But those who exalt themselves will be humbled, and those who humble themselves will be exalted."*

In today's church culture many pastors have a Pharisee complex. Intentionally or not, they maximize the distance between pulpit and pew as they preach passionately and instruct the flock. Their messages either dredge the depths of theology with expository preaching or skim the crest of popular culture with topical treatises. But either extreme can easily miss the point. As important as sound biblical teaching is, if the pastor does not equip the people to go make disciples, the church is not functioning correctly. God's heart behind pastoral ministry is to equip regular people to go out and help other people pursue him. Anything short of that is pharisaical.

What message would it have sent if Jesus chose Pharisees instead of fishermen? The early church would have looked very different. Instead of a movement for the masses, it would have been relegated to the smart, rich and powerful. It would have elevated head knowledge above heart obedience. It would have made the early Christian message inaccessible to the average guy. And it would have created a massive divide between qualified teachers and the average Christian.

It might have looked like many of our churches today.[4]

Jesus picked fishermen instead of Pharisees as a reminder for the church in all ages. Professional preachers don't make a church healthy. Regular people being "fishers of men" - that's the church Jesus envisioned.[5]

---

4 http://www.pursuegod.org/church-is-more-than-a-sermon/
5 https://www.pursuegodnetwork.org/what-is-a-discipleship-culture/

Ch 3. The World Just Got Complicated

In the mid 1400's, a German goldsmith named Johannes Gutenberg created an innovation that would forever alter the course of history. With his invention of the printing press, mass communication was born. Prior to that time, information and ideas were spread slowly, often orally from person to person. With the advent of the printing press, literacy rates would rise and information would begin to flow like never before in history. Knowledge was now available to the common man.

It soon affected the culture of Europe. When Martin Luther published his 95 Theses against the corruption in the Roman Catholic church, word spread like wildfire. The Protestant Reformation took off with the help of this nascent mass media industry, and a new movement of churches was born. With the printing press, corrupt institutional authority was challenged and great leaders everywhere were given a platform to share their message.

Today, we have experienced a second information revolution. With the internet, the platform has gotten exponentially bigger. Now anyone can share their ideas and opinions, and the effect is staggering. Consider these stats:

- *The famous "Gutenberg Bible" initiated the printing revolution in Europe, with a total of less than 200 copies sold. In 2016, basketball star LeBron James had over 31 million Twitter followers.*
- *Between 1518 and 1520, Martin Luther distributed over 300,000 copies of his tracts and ignited the Reformation. In 2016, the Huffington Post had an estimated 110 million unique visitors every month.*

- *During his lifetime in the early 1500's, Erasmus sold over 750,000 copies of his works. In 2016, it took just 88 days for songwriter Adele's music video "Hello" to reach 1 billion unique views on YouTube.*

The changes we've seen in our culture over the last 500 years are soon to be dwarfed by the changes we will see in the next 50. If the church is to still be relevant for our kids and grandkids, we better start working right again.

The Trillion Choice Universe

When I was young, life was pretty simple. As painful as it is to admit, I watched The Brady Bunch most days right before dinner, as did almost all of my friends. When I did research for a homework assignment at school, I went to the library to wade through unwieldy encyclopedias. And playing a video game was simple choice between Atari and Intellivision.

Today, my kids are growing up in a completely different world. On Netflix alone they have access to over 100,000 video titles. Wikipedia in the English language has over 5 million articles, and by 2013 Google had indexed over 30 trillion pages of information online. And online gaming options are legion. All of this is literally at the fingertips of anyone with a smartphone or laptop.

We live in a trillion choice universe, and Google helped to create it. Google, of course, makes no judgment on the information that it is collecting. It's an equal opportunity distributor, putting out the ideas and philosophies of the world's experts alongside the everyday musings and opinions of average people. The net effect is information overload. If the strategy of Satan in the Dark Ages was to withhold information from the masses, his strategy in the information age is to obscure the truth in a sea of ideas. How much of the world's information and opinions will Google index and make available to us? All of it.[6]

The Google Generation

As a result, the Google generation has no idea which way is up. The proliferation of opinions has made every speaker a pundit and every listener a consumer. But few people have a grid for weighing all of the options. And with so many voices, who decides what is true? In today's schools kids are taught that all opinions are valid. So how do kids decide what to believe? It's a frightening new twist on an age-old problem.

This became clear to me when I talked recently with some old friends from youth group. These men and women are faithful church goers, doing their best to raise their kids in an increasingly secular culture. When our conversation wandered onto the topic of homosexuality and the Bible, there was a split opinion. Few of them knew how to think biblically about the issue, but they were well-versed in the talking points of popular opinion. Though they knew the biblical perspective on the matter, they were unsure how - *or if* - to articulate it.

This is not a new challenge for the church today, but it is unique. Even back in the time of the judges, everyone did what was right in their own eyes. But the difference is this: today, people have so much more content right in front of their eyes. The challenge for church leaders today is not too far removed from the mission of Google. Google's goal was to organize the world's information. If we are to create disciples who make disciples, our job as leaders is to help people access the truth in a sea of opinions.

---

[6] http://www.pursuegod.org/dangerous-ideas-grid-1/

Judges 17:6 *In those days Israel had no king; all the people did whatever seemed right in their own eyes.*

Google Think

Google a random topic and you will get thousands of search results from all around the country and the world. Have you ever thought about how the information is organized, and in what order? Google's algorithms are complicated and always changing, but the bottom line is that your search results are a combination of the most popular information and your own personal preferences as tracked by Google. Google's algorithms anticipate and interpret our needs and opinions. The net effect is that Google helps us find information that we *want*, but not necessarily information we can *trust*.

Google makes a basic assumption about people: The crowd is wise and basically good. With every click, the crowd is voting on the most relevant and popular answers, and those answers are taken to be true. In the world of Google, merit is determined by crowd appeal. To Google, truth is democratic. Good companies have great customer service, but Google takes it a step further. For Google, the customer is in charge. Google users don't just consume a product; they create the product. They shape the way Google interacts with them. Google learns from them, responds to them, and creates the world they want to see.

Author Jeff Jarvis insightfully observed, "At Google, we are God and our data is the Bible." The brilliance of Google is to track my searches and preferences to create a digital world that revolves around me.

Now don't misunderstand my rant. I love Google. I use it every day of my life. The incredible tool of Google is not the problem. Google's goal of organizing the world's information is impressively humanitarian. Its desire to give the customer what he or she wants is noteworthy. The problem is not Google. The internet is user-sensitive, and the users are the problem.[7]

According to the Bible, people are *not* basically good. Because of this simple fact, crowdsourcing the truth is a horrible idea. If you want to learn how to fix a toilet, Google will do just fine. But if you want to know how to get to heaven, you had better get your information from the right source.

The YouTube Effect

February 1st, 2004 is a day that will live on in infamy. It was Super Bowl Sunday, and the game pitted the New England Patriots against the Carolina Panthers. New England ended up winning the game, but that wasn't the true history-making event of the day. This was the Super Bowl where Justin Timberlake and Janet Jackson performed at halftime, creating a media uproar with the infamous "wardrobe malfunction".

Don't Google it.

The incident made "Janet Jackson" the most searched term in internet history. And when Jawed Karim, a young employee at PayPal, struggled to find the video online, the idea for YouTube was born.

Here's how the site works. Go to youtube.com and start browsing videos. You can find anything from cats to education to comedy to complete randomness. YouTube is a massive video library where anyone can create their own channel and post videos for free. Just

---

[7] https://www.flextalk.org/what-the-internet-is-doing-to-our-brains/

two decades ago only massive media companies could broadcast video content to the world. Now, with YouTube, even YOU can.

Here are some helpful statistics (from YouTube.com):

- YouTube has over a billion users — almost one-third of all people on the Internet — and everyday people watch hundreds of millions of hours on YouTube and generate billions of views.
- YouTube overall, and even YouTube on mobile alone, reaches more 18-49 year-olds than any cable network in the U.S.
- Growth in watch time on YouTube has accelerated and is up at least 50% year over year for three straight years.
- The number of people watching YouTube per day is up 40% year over year since March 2014.

YouTube is still in its infancy, but already more people today get their ideas and opinions from its channels than they do from the Bible. By a longshot.

"YouTube is everything," my daughter said nonchalantly. We were driving along the highway, having one of those father-daughter conversations.

"Yeah," I said, not really listening. "Wait... what did you say?"

"YouTube is everything," she repeated. "It's what everyone watches. All of my friends are on YouTube all day."

I felt old.

"So that's still a thing?" I asked.

"Of course," she explained. "Pay attention to the commercials on TV. Most of those people you don't recognize are YouTubers."

"Just people who randomly started their own YouTube channels?"

"Yep." She was a young woman of few words.

"And they have enough subscribers to appeal to a national crowd?"

"Oh yeah," she said. "Some of them have millions."

I couldn't process it. Just an average person with a simple camera. Competing with the massive media outlets.

"Like I said," she concluded. "YouTube is everything."

Everyone YouTubes

There's something here to be learned, especially for pastors and leaders in the church. YouTube is elevating regular people to superstar status. It is giving everyone a platform, and people are taking advantage of it. Everyone and their brother is starting a YouTube channel to show their life or share their opinion or spread what they're most passionate about.

Everyone but Christians.

Surf the most popular YouTube channels and one thing will become painfully clear. The most creative, innovative, and even educational channels are hosted by secular ideologues who are spreading their version of reality. These are not trained professionals. They are just passionate everyday people who feel empowered to spread their vision to anyone who will listen. They are street prophets and crack philosophers who think that they have something worth saying. And so they say it, on video.

Wait a second. Does this storyline sound familiar? Open the Bible and you'll see that this was the heart and mission of the early Christians. They were empowered to spread their vision. They believed that their message was worth hearing, so they took it to the street and put it in front of anyone who would listen. They were usually not afraid, and when they were they prayed harder for boldness to spread the gospel. Though they had no internet or smartphone or worldwide platform, they had passion. And they had the mandate from Jesus himself to go make disciples. So they did, without video.

Why is the secular crowd more passionate and committed to sharing their message than followers of Jesus today? Why the big switch? I think I know at least part of the answer, and it's why the church is broken. Christians go to church and hear a message from the pastor behind the pulpit. That's his job, not theirs. They don't have the burden of sharing the truth, but simply come to church and listen to the sermon. The pastor is the professional. If somebody is to come to faith, the pastor will be the one to get him there. If somebody has a question about life or marriage or theology, the pastor stands ready to swoop in and have a conversation. That's his job.

Secularists are not programmed to think this way. They don't go to church and they certainly don't listen to pastors. Somehow, this gives them a greater sense of empowerment. They are free to share their views and their perspectives. They can speak with confidence about what they believe to be true, and nobody will rebuke them in the name of Jesus or correct them in case their theology is off a bit. YouTube is dominated by secularists because they are the ones who feel most emboldened to share their opinion. Christians hesitate either because they don't have a deep-rooted conviction about God's opinion or they simply don't feel that it is their place or responsibility to share it.

The net effect is that everyone is making disciples, except the ones who should be.

I'm not suggesting that every Christian should buy a camera and start a YouTube channel, although that wouldn't be a half bad idea. The bigger point is that we as Christians need to feel empowered to share the truth of a biblical worldview even if we don't have a degree to back it up. The real lesson of YouTube is that people are interested in people, especially the passionate ones. It's time for Christians to step up and be passionate about Jesus. We don't have to be obnoxious or arrogant or rude, but we have every right to be confident, clear and compelling about how we see the world. Our kids and neighbors need us to act like we believe what the Bible says, even if it goes against what the whole world is saying.

Especially if it goes against what the whole world is saying.

The world just got complicated, and information is coming at us a mile a minute. The church that Jesus envisioned would be ready to join in, leveraging the internet age and empowering believers everywhere to get the word out.[8]

---

[8] http://www.pursuegod.org/going-out-grid-5/

Ch 4. Cows Make Milk

"So tell me how the dairy business works," I said to Chad, a long time friend and a successful dairy farmer. I had been mentoring him over the phone for several months, and at the time we were covering basic leadership topics.

I clarified, "What's the bottom line for a dairy man?"

"Milk production," he answered without hesitation. "More milk per cow. That's the bottom line. It's all about maximizing efficiency."

"How do you make that happen?" I asked.

"Technology, genetic testing, breeding, nutrition. Everything we do, we do to make better cows."

"And how do you define a better cow?"

"More milk." Chad had simple clarity. That's why he was so successful.

"So what do you do with a cow that doesn't produce?"

He laughed. "Really? Are you going to make me say it?"

I said it for him. "Off to the meat market, huh?"

"Yeah," Chad replied. "You'll eat that one for dinner someday."

"You won't just keep it on the farm like a pet?"

"Ha! No way," he laughed. "We've only got room for 2000 cows. Every spot counts. We need to get the most production out of every cow we keep on the line."

"And what happens to the guy who doesn't run his dairy like that?" I asked.

Chad had seen it happen. "That guy goes out of business."

Non-Producers

The church that Jesus envisioned is a movement that produces disciples who produce more disciples. Everyone carries their own weight and pitches in to work for the Kingdom of God. Every believer feels the responsibility to make disciples. When Jesus explained this to his disciples, he used imagery that they were sure to understand.

> ***John 15:1-2*** *""I am the true grapevine, and my Father is the gardener. He cuts off every branch of mine that doesn't produce fruit, and he prunes the branches that do bear fruit so they will produce even more."*

Jesus wasn't messing around. He only had a few more days with his disciples, and he wanted to make sure they were ready for their job. If they didn't get his picture of discipleship, then the church they were tasked to start wouldn't get it either.

But most churches today have lost sight of the mission of Jesus. We have slipped from a producer mentality to a consumer one. Most Sundays we pile our families into minivans and drive to church to listen as a professional pastor delivers a polished sermon. Then we nod and smile and thank him for the talk, and we get back in our minivans and forget all about it. He did his job, and that's the end of it.

Americans are accustomed to the consumer mentality. We go to the big box stores and get pitched the newest products. We sit down for lunch and get great service from start to finish - or else they lose our business. And we go to church with the same mentality. The videos, the music, the sermon - all of it is product. And we are ever evaluating, ready to take our business elsewhere if need be.[9]

Long-time Christians are famous for their consumer mentality. "The sermons aren't deep enough. The music isn't moving enough." These comments are dead giveaways that a Christian has started missing the point. Consumers are looking to be fed rather than to feed. They are viewing their church experience as a product, rather than seeing themselves as a producer of disciples. Sadly, the church seems like a Walmart Superstore, with all the spiritual milk, meat and gadgets available to the people. And God's people are the shoppers who come to consume and take advantage of all the weekly specials - only to come back next week and see what's new on the shelves..

> *"People looking for handouts just drive me nuts," Jacob said, fired up. It was my men's group and we were talking about givers versus takers in society.*
>
> *"I don't have a problem if someone is really in need," he continued. "But it's the entitlement attitude that I can't stand."*
>
> *The men in the group had a variety of political perspectives. But we were all middle class, tax-paying citizens.*

---

[9] http://www.pursuegod.org/three-types-of-almost-disciples/

"I can't stand a leech," chimed in another guy.

"Who are the leeches at church?" I asked, turning the conversation. "Spiritually, I mean?"

Silence. These guys were sharp, and they knew where I was going.

"The guys who don't make disciples," Jacob answered, sheepishly.

"That's right," I smiled. "I can't stand those guys."

The Customer Conundrum

For the church today, we are struggling to answer a basic business question. Who are our customers? Take a look at most churches, and the answer seems obvious: Christians. Consumer Christianity makes the disciples of Jesus into the customers and the leaders of the church into the customer service representatives.

But Jesus envisioned something different.

In Jesus' model, the customers are not the ones we would expect. Jesus went among the people of Israel, inviting them to be a part of his Kingdom. They were the ones who already felt they were on the "inside", and they took their relationship with God for granted. Many church-goers today are in the same position. But Jesus made a startling point with his parable.

> ***Luke 14:21-24*** *"The servant returned and told his master what they had said. His master was furious and said, 'Go quickly into the streets and alleys of the town and invite the poor, the crippled, the blind, and the lame.' After the servant had done this, he reported, 'There is still room for more.' So his master said, 'Go out into the country lanes and behind the hedges and urge anyone you find to come, so that the house will be full. For none of those I first invited will get even the smallest taste of my banquet.'"*

Our customers are the people on the outside of the church, not the ones on the inside. The Apostle Peter affirmed this simple truth after he preached his first sermon. The listening crowd was cut to the heart, and they asked Peter what they should do in response to the gospel.

> ***Acts 2:38-39*** *Peter replied, "Each of you must repent of your sins and turn to God, and be baptized in the name of Jesus Christ for the forgiveness of your sins. Then you will receive the gift of the Holy Spirit. This promise is to you, to your children, and to those far away—all who have been called by the Lord our God."*

The promise was for them and their children and "for all who are far off". Everyone on the outside was a customer, and the people on the inside had a tremendous gift to offer.

Later in the book of Acts Peter himself was shocked to learn the full extent of this statement. Sent by God to the house of Cornelius, a Gentile who feared the Lord, Peter preached to the family about Jesus. To his surprise they received the message, and God invited them into the community of faith with the same sign he had given the Jewish believers earlier in Acts.

> ***Acts 10:44-47*** *Even as Peter was saying these things, the Holy Spirit fell upon all who were listening to the message. The Jewish believers who came with Peter were amazed that the gift of the Holy Spirit had been poured out on the Gentiles, too. For they heard them speaking in other tongues and praising God. Then Peter asked, "Can anyone object to their being baptized, now that they have received the Holy Spirit just as we did?"*

The mystery of the gospel is that Jesus offers the same salvation to both Jew and Gentile. The whole world is a customer for what the church has to offer, and they remain customers until the day they become followers of Jesus. On that day they become producers, called to make disciples like the rest of us.

What about your church? Is it as focused as the early church? Does it look outward, looking to reach the non-members? Or is confused about who the real customers are?

> *Amazon.com was just a few years old and still an online bookseller. Jeff Bezos was at the helm, and he sent out his now-famous shareholder report in 1997. In one section he outlined his company's commitment to its values.*
>
>> *"Because of our emphasis on the long term, we may make decisions and weigh tradeoffs differently than some companies. Accordingly, we want to share with you our fundamental management and decision-making approach so that you, our shareholders, may confirm that it is consistent with your investment philosophy: We will continue to focus relentlessly on our customers...."*

Customers, wrote Bezos, would be the first and most valued priority. It was the cornerstone of Bezos' unconventional leadership style.

Within a decade Amazon.com would become the world's largest online retailer, making Jeff Bezos one of the wealthiest men in the world.

Disciples of Jesus are not supposed to be consumers. We are called to be the servers at the table, not the ones eating. Jesus dramatically illustrated this truth at the last supper with his disciples.

> **John 13:3-5** *Jesus knew that the Father had given him authority over everything and that he had come from God and would return to God. So he got up from the table, took off his robe, wrapped a towel around his waist, and poured water into a basin. Then he began to wash the disciples' feet, drying them with the towel he had around him.*

Christians today are more likely to know the chapter and verse of this famous story than to understand its meaning for the church today. It's because Jesus had authority that he became a servant. This is the way of the Kingdom of God: the most mature ones are always looking to serve. Their focus is outward and they do everything they can to help the ones who are less mature.

> **John 13:12-15** *After washing their feet, he put on his robe again and sat down and asked, "Do you understand what I was doing? You call me 'Teacher' and 'Lord,' and you are right, because that's what I am. And since I, your Lord and Teacher,*

have washed your feet, you ought to wash each other's feet. I have given you an example to follow. Do as I have done to you.

When a mature follower of Jesus recognizes her calling to serve others, it extends to the most central mission of the church. She becomes a disciple-maker, looking especially to the people outside the church walls.

They are the real customers.

"Are you the senior pastor here?" The visitor asked me in the lobby of the church. I braced myself for one of those conversations I'd had many times before.

"Well, we don't really use that kind of terminology around here," I replied cautiously.

"You know what I mean," he said with a smile. "Who's in charge?"

I took a deep breath. I could tell from this guy's Bible that he was a long-time Christian. And from his accent I discerned that he had just arrived from the Bible Belt.

"Well I planted the church, if that helps," I said, giving in. "But we take a team approach around here."

"Great. I'd like to start a Bible study that goes deeper. I led one at my last church." He really wasn't trying to be arrogant. He wanted to serve along the lines of his gifting, and he felt he was gifted at teaching. But I knew we weren't on the same page, and I wanted to gently help him see the difference.

"What do you mean by 'deeper'?" I asked.

"You know, something with a little more meat. Something for a more mature Christian."

I countered: "How do you define 'mature'?"

Silence. He never really had to put it in words.

"Well, someone who really knows how to study the Bible. You know, digs in."

"Yeah. We define Christian maturity a little differently," I said, getting to the punchline. "We believe the most mature Christians engage with people who are far from God. That's where the best kind of discipleship starts - on the outside of the church. Mature Christians don't just lead Bible studies for the people who are already here."

Again, silence.

"I'm not saying Bible studies are bad. I love them." I really meant what I was saying. "It's just that once people start defining maturity like that, they usually become pretty useless as far as our mission."

He didn't seem to be buying it. So I went to the litmus test.

"Have you ever helped someone become a Christian?" I asked.

"No, not really," he finally admitted. "I lead Bible studies."

Now I was silent. I don't think he was getting it.

Consumer Christians today talk about getting to the "meat" of deeper truths and going beyond the "milk" of basic teachings. But even Jesus defined what he saw as the real "meat" of a mature pursuer of God. After sharing about the Kingdom of God with the woman at the well, he turned to his 12 disciples:

> ***John 4:34-35*** *Then Jesus explained: "My nourishment comes from doing the will of God, who sent me, and from finishing his work. You know the saying, 'Four months between planting and harvest.' But I say, wake up and look around. The fields are already ripe for harvest.*

The only solid food that Jesus needed was to be obedient to the Father and to accomplish his mission on earth. A mature Christian doesn't need to get any deeper than this. The fields are white for harvest and the redeeming work of Jesus is already done. Now we just need a few "deep" Christians to go beyond consumer Christianity and actually help people who are far from God.

The church needs more disciple-makers, not just more Bible study leaders. This is the church that Jesus envisioned.

Knowledge that Puffs Up

It's not that God doesn't want us to listen to great sermons or go to in-depth Bible studies. Bible knowledge is good. After all, saving faith starts with having the right knowledge about Jesus and sin. A vibrant spiritual life brings us deeper into knowledge, leading us to understand the finer points of theology and Christian living. But like anything good, knowledge can be used for bad. This is especially true in religious circles. Paul reminded the dysfunctional church in Corinth of this:

> ***1 Corinthians 8:1-3*** *Now regarding your question about food that has been offered to idols. Yes, we know that "we all have knowledge" about this issue. But while knowledge makes us feel important, it is love that strengthens the church. Anyone who claims to know all the answers doesn't really know very much. But the person who loves God is the one whom God recognizes.*

Here was the question, in a nutshell: Was it OK to eat food that had been sacrificed to idols? Some of the Christians had a weak conscience about it, not confident that it was a God-honoring activity. Others knew the truth about idols - that they were nothing and therefore the meat was not defiled. This second group was the one that had "knowledge". The truth had dawned on them, and they were further down the road in this area of faith than the other group whose conscience was weak. Paul acknowledged this, but he had a bigger point to make: even though you're right, don't eat the meat. Don't let your superior knowledge make you arrogant and dismissive of the person who doesn't see it your way yet. Love that person, and do everything in your power to build that person's faith.

It's a clear case of the Christian who is farther along proving his maturity by deferring to those who were further back.

The early followers of Jesus didn't have the temptation to be "puffed up" with knowledge like we do today. The truth is, the average Christian today has far more Bible knowledge than those people. Think about it. How many Bible studies did they attend on a weekly basis? They had no Bibles to study, at least not like we do! Do you think they even had a personal copy of the Torah? So how much "Bible" knowledge did the first disciples even have? We can at least begin to answer this question. They knew the gospel. They knew the Greatest Commandment. And they knew the Great Commission. And so they obeyed. They shared the simple truths that they understood, pointing people to the Jesus that they personally knew. Consider Peter's first sermon:

> ***Acts 2:22-24,36*** *"People of Israel, listen! God publicly endorsed Jesus the Nazarene by doing powerful miracles, wonders, and signs through him, as you well know. But God knew what would happen, and his prearranged plan was carried out when Jesus was betrayed. With the help of lawless Gentiles, you nailed him to a cross and killed him. But God released him from the horrors of death and raised him back to life, for death could not keep him in its grip.... "So let everyone in Israel know for certain that God has made this Jesus, whom you crucified, to be both Lord and Messiah!"*

Peter was not trained in preaching or well-versed in theology to the extent that seminarians are today. He walked with Jesus for three years, learning the basic framework for a pursuit of God and observing as Jesus made it clear through simple stories. Peter heard the truth like a fisherman would, and he learned how to communicate it to other regular people.

Meanwhile, the Pharisees had heads filled with knowledge and theology, and they lorded it over the people. They loved their complicated system with its rules and regulations, and they made it difficult for anyone to get in. Jesus often spoke out against them.

> ***Matthew 23:13-15*** *"What sorrow awaits you teachers of religious law and you Pharisees. Hypocrites! For you shut the door of the Kingdom of Heaven in people's faces. You won't go in yourselves, and you don't let others enter either. "What sorrow awaits you teachers of religious law and you Pharisees. Hypocrites! For you cross land and sea to make one convert, and then you turn that person into twice the child of hell you yourselves are!"*

To our shame, many "deep" Christians today look more like a Pharisee than a fisherman. They fill their heads with knowledge, puffing themselves up with spiritual arrogance and separating themselves from the crowd of "normal" people. They develop and speak their own language, making it harder and harder for the uninitiated to understand the simple gospel - if they would even bother to share it in the first place.

Sadly, some of these Christians are leaders in our churches. Their heads are filled with knowledge but their hearts are complacent toward lost and sinful people. And the great irony, for many of them, is that they think *they* are the mature ones. But the Bible tells a different story. Consider Paul's words to the dysfunctional Corinthians church:

> ***1 Corinthians 3:1-5*** *But I, brothers, could not address you as spiritual people, but as people of the flesh, as infants in Christ. I fed you with milk, not solid food, for you were not ready for it. And even now you are not yet ready, for you are still of the flesh. For while there is jealousy and strife among you, are you not of the flesh and behaving only in a human way? For when one says, "I follow Paul," and another, "I follow Apollos," are you not being merely human?*

Paul is describing consumer Christians, people in the church who loved their preachers. They had their favorites, yet they were missing the point. Paul said they were spiritual babies.

So it all comes back to the same principle that Paul taught in Ephesians 4 and that Jesus taught throughout his ministry. Real Christian maturity is evidenced by a believer loving people enough to help them pursue God. It's not just about your favorite preacher or Bible study.

The Greatest Commandment

Two thousand years ago, the religious leaders of the day asked Jesus a simple question. They had broken the church by their failure to help people pursue God, and now they tried to trap Jesus with their lies.

> ***Matthew 22:35-40 (ESV)*** *And one of [the Pharisees], a lawyer, asked him a question to test him. "Teacher, which is the great commandment in the Law?" And he said to him, "You shall love the Lord your God with all your heart and with all your soul and with all your mind. This is the great and first commandment. And a second is like it: You shall love your neighbor as yourself. On these two commandments depend all the Law and the Prophets."*

Jesus didn't hesitate to give his simple answer. It was clear to him what the meaning of life was for a pursuer of God, and for the church of God: love God first and love people second. They were two sides of the same coin, inseparable in essence and practice. A church filled with authentic Christ-followers will embrace this as the fundamental framework for doing church right.[10]

The church may be the only organization in the world that genuinely exists for its non-members, and this is what Jesus was getting at with the second part of his answer. For a church to be truly healthy, it has to love people. And the most loving thing a church can do is to *personally* make disciples. The church is called out from the world to join Jesus on his mission in the world.[11]

---

[10] http://www.pursuegod.org/5-lame-excuses-not-to-mentor/
[11] http://www.pursuegod.org/you-were-born-to-reproduce/

Luke 19:10 *"For the Son of Man came to seek and to save the lost."*

Jesus taught that a good shepherd would leave the 99 sheep who are safely in the pen to go after the one who has wandered out into danger. That's his missional philosophy. Yet today, too many churches are holy huddles - gathering privately with each other and connecting in their safe community to the neglect of the one(s) out in the dangerous world. This is not the church that Jesus envisioned, and it is the primary reason the church is broken today.

"Can you pray for my husband? He's struggling with porn again." The young woman in front of me had been attending since our church was very small. I knew her well, and my heart broke for her situation.

"Of course," I said, grabbing her hand. I prayed and she thanked me. But I felt compelled to do more.

"Is he coming to church any more?" I asked, searching for a solution.

"No, not really," she replied through tears.

"Are you guys connected to a small group?"

"No, he won't come."

"What about you? Are you connected beyond Sunday?"

"I can't make it on Thursday nights, though I'd like to," she replied. "It's just too busy with work and the kids."

My heart broke for her. I knew that a sermon wasn't enough. She needed to be connected to someone, but we didn't offer that.

"See you next week," I called out as she walked away.

Then she was gone.

Church Is More Than a Sermon

It's hard to love someone through a sermon. Some preachers are warmer and more inspiring than others, but no one can properly meet the needs and answer the questions of every listener through an on-stage monologue. That's simply a limitation of preaching. Public preaching certainly has its place in the life of the church, but it's not the magic bullet for healthy ministry.

Preaching is speaking truth to a crowd. Discipling is speaking truth in love.[12]

That's why Paul said the pastors had to equip the people to minister. His idea was that everyone would go out and feel empowered to help the people in their world to hear and apply the truth of the Bible. A sermon can introduce a biblical truth to the mind and heart of a seeker. But a personal conversation is the typical mechanism God uses to minister his message to the world. It's incarnational. It's love.

We find this principle in our Ephesians 4 passage. Take a look:

---

12 http://www.pursuegod.org/church-is-more-than-a-sermon/

Ephesians 4:15-16 *Instead, we will speak the truth in love, growing in every way more and more like Christ, who is the head of his body, the church. He makes the whole body fit together perfectly. As each part does its own special work, it helps the other parts grow, so that the whole body is healthy, growing and full of love.*

If the pastor is the only one speaking truth, the church can't build the loving community that Jesus envisioned. But when regular people are empowered to "speak the truth in love" - at home, in the neighborhood, in small groups, everywhere - the church can't help but grow into a vibrant, healthy community.

"We need to talk," Ryan said, walking in for our weekly mentoring meeting.

It had turned into more of a coaching meeting. He was already mentoring other people in his world, and we usually talked about how those relationships were going.

"I'm frustrated with Jason," he continued.

"What's up?" I asked. "Is he flaking out on you?"

"No, not at all. We meet every week, and our conversations are always great." Ryan paused. "It's just that I can't get the guy to come to church."

I started to understand.

"He has trusted Jesus for salvation, right?" I asked.

"Yes."

"And he is honoring God in his life?"

"Right."

"Is he mentoring anyone yet?"

"Yes, he's trying. He's bringing it home to his wife and kids." Ryan explained. "But they're still Mormon, so he doesn't want to freak them out by coming to a Christian church."

"Well that's great," I assured him. "He's learning how to love people. He's preferring their needs above his. It's like speaking the right truth at the right time."

"Yeah, but doesn't he have to come to church?" Ryan asked.

"Listen," I explained. "If he came to Alpine, we would be trying to get him into a mentoring relationship anyway. You're already doing the main thing. Connection to our church is important, and that will come soon enough. For now, just keep mentoring."

Ryan's eyes brightened.

"You're already winning," I said. "Discipling is the win."

Jesus envisioned a church that cares more about people than institutions or structures. It's a movement of disciples who care enough about people on the outside to actually invest in them personally. It defines maturity not in terms of Bible knowledge, but in terms of loving people enough to help them pursue God.

Ch 5. Defining "Disciple"

So we knew that our church was broken, and that finding a simple strategy for making disciples was the thing to fix it. But before we could create the strategy, we had to clear up our terms. What, exactly, was a disciple? If we didn't know what our end product looked like, how could we effectively make one? We had to define "disciple," and we started on it right away.

Our first attempt to define a disciple was to come up with a list of 12 things we believed should characterize the life of every biblical Christian. Later we narrowed it down to 10. We put it together in a booklet we called "Foundations" and printed thousands of copies. It was a hit. Creating a clear pathway for people who wanted to pursue God opened the floodgates for faith. Hundreds of people began making commitments to Christ after going through our Foundations class. The fruit of our labor for years had suddenly ripened, catalyzed by our simple tool and straightforward process.

But there was still a problem. Once people were done with the simple Foundations series, they weren't sure what to do next. Some of them joined a small group. Others started serving in the church. It was good, but it wasn't great. We knew we were still missing something. Our process lacked clarity, and our tools were incomplete. People were still dependent on the pastors to make disciples. We went back to the drawing board.

Our definition for disciple needed to be simpler. Foundations had three sections. In 101, people learned the gospel and were given an opportunity to respond to it. In 201 we listed the 10 things that we believed should show up in a God-honoring life. In 301 we challenged our readers with a 6-month New Testament reading plan. It was helpful, but clunky. Ask someone at Victory to describe the Christian life and the answer was simple: honor God, make disciples. Ask an Alpiner to define a believer, and you'd get a blank stare or a laundry list. There had to be a better way.

"Simple can be harder than complex," wrote Steve Jobs. "You have to work hard to get your thinking clean to make it simple."

When Jobs started Apple, he had a vision for a beautiful personal computer. He wasn't the greatest engineer or programmer in the burgeoning tech industry of the 1980's, but he had an edge that set him apart.

"Simplicity is the ultimate sophistication," he said. His goal was to take something complex and nerdy - the computer - and make it accessible to the average person. He focused on innovation and usability, popularizing the drag-and-click user interfaces on his early Apple computers.

He took those same principles to the next level with the innovations of the iPod, the iPad and the iPhone.

"Design is a funny word," he later reflected. "Some people think design means how it looks. But of course, if you dig deeper, it's really how it works."

As we struggled to define the core attributes of a disciple, we hit upon a simple idea.

"What if we can combine both the form and the function," we thought. "Let's simplify what it means to pursue God and give people a visual to help them see how it actually works."

We came up with a 3-part picture of what it means to pursue God. We wanted it to be biblical and memorable, easy enough for our own children to understand and live out. What we came up with became the new framework for our Faith 101 series[13] and the entire discipleship library we were developing. Here's the picture:

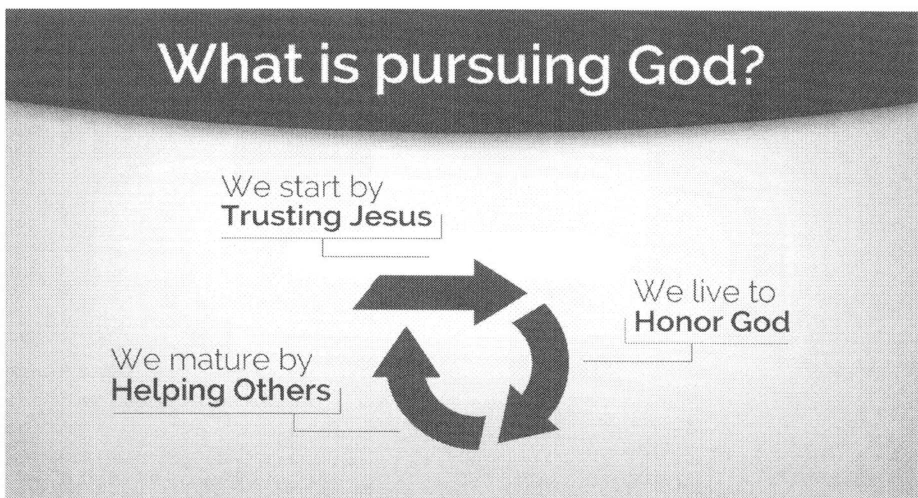

The pursuer of God does three things: trusts Jesus, honors God, and helps others pursue God (ie, makes disciples). Drawing these three activities in a circle allowed us to illustrate that these activities never end, either for the disciple-maker or the new disciple. It's a beautiful, reproducible system loop. We called this all-in disciple a "full circle" Christian. With this level of simplicity and clarity, it was easy for us to define the win, whether for a church, a small group or a family. The ultimate win is one more person going "full circle". And when that person wins, we are set up to win again and again. It combines form and function for the Christian life, and it's the kind of viral faith that Jesus envisioned all along.

---

[13] http://www.pursuegod.org/faith-101/

This became the simple framework that would propel the rest of our system for discipleship. Let's break it down.

Arrow 1: Trusting Jesus

The initial and most fundamental stage of discipleship is trusting Jesus.[14] This is the heart of the gospel, and it's the starting point for any person's relationship with God. Trusting Jesus can take two primary forms.

Trusting his perspective. Everyone has opinions, but when we come to Christ we are called to drop our own opinions in favor of adopting God's view of the world. Sin, in fact, can be simply defined as trusting and acting on our own opinions and feelings rather than trusting and acting on God's truth. Adam and Eve sinned in the garden in this way, and every time we sin we're doing the same thing.

> ***Genesis 3:6-7*** *The woman was convinced. She saw that the tree was beautiful and its fruit looked delicious, and she wanted the wisdom it would give her. So she took some of the fruit and ate it. Then she gave some to her husband, who was with her, and he ate it, too. At that moment their eyes were opened, and they suddenly felt shame at their nakedness. So they sewed fig leaves together to cover themselves.*

God had already told the first humans what the rules were. In his kindness he gave them every other tree in the garden. But they questioned his perspective and authority. And in the end, they elevated their opinion about God's truth.

Trusting God's perspective is the heart of repentance. When we repent, we are showing our willingness to turn from our way to God's

---

[14] http://www.pursuegod.org/how-to-start-a-pursuit-of-god/

way. We are submitting ourselves to Jesus as Lord of our lives. We are confessing our inadequacies and our sins - literally "saying the same thing" about our sins that God is already saying. We are aligning ourselves with God, giving up the fight to be in charge.

And once we have the attitude of repentance, we are in position to experience the second side of trusting Jesus.

Trusting his power. When we see God for who he really is - and therefore we see ourselves for who we really are - we recognize our deep need for him. By nature we are impotent, and our generous estimate of our own power must be seen for the sham that it truly is. We are not God. We have no real claim to his authority. We have power over nothing and no one.

The prophet Isaiah had this experience when he came face-to-face with God.

> ***Isaiah 6:4-5*** *Their voices shook the Temple to its foundations, and the entire building was filled with smoke. Then I said, "It's all over! I am doomed, for I am a sinful man. I have filthy lips, and I live among a people with filthy lips. Yet I have seen the King, the Lord of Heaven's Armies."*

Isaiah couldn't stand in the presence of the omnipotent God. Confronted with the splendor of God's holiness, Isaiah confessed for himself and his people. It reminds us of the reaction of the Jewish crowd after Peter's first sermon. It was the opening act of the early church, and God did a supernatural work in the hearts of the hearers that day.

> ***Acts 2:37-39*** *Peter's words pierced their hearts, and they said to him and to the other apostles, "Brothers, what should we do?" Peter replied, "Each of you must repent of your sins and turn to*

God, and be baptized in the name of Jesus Christ for the forgiveness of your sins. Then you will receive the gift of the Holy Spirit. This promise is to you, to your children, and to those far away—all who have been called by the Lord our God."

This passage illustrates perfectly the first phase of discipleship: trusting in Jesus for salvation. The people were "cut to the heart" and trusted God's perspective as Peter made it plain, and in their response they trusted Christ's power to save them from their sins.

"I'd love to talk through some faith topics," Lexi said. She and Sam would be getting married soon, and we were covering our typical premarital lessons. But as we had seen so many times before, it often opened the door to deeper topics.

"That's great. Have you guys taken Faith 101 yet?" I asked.

"No, but we've been talking about it," Sam replied. They had been coming to church for a few months now, but they hadn't yet experienced the "faith moment".

Lexi grew up Mormon, and her whole life she was trained to read their scriptures. But that didn't typically include the Bible, so she was eager to learn more about the historical Jesus. Sam, on the other hand, grew up in a home without religion.

Lexi was hungry for the truth of the Bible. Sam was a little hesitant.

"Alright," I said. "Why don't we pause with our premarital series for a few while. We've got time. Let's start on Faith 101 next week - can you be ready for the first lesson?"

"We'll be ready!" They said.

The next week they returned, ready for the conversation. They hadn't just prepped for the first lesson on trusting Jesus. They dug into all of the related topics and were eager to talk.

We covered some of the questions together, and it was clear that the Holy Spirit had opened their eyes to the truth of the gospel. By the end of that meeting, they were both ready to accept Christ. We prayed together, and their journey had begun.

Trusting Jesus isn't just something we do to kickstart our relationship with God. The reality is that we'll never be done with this first phase. In every new situation, whether in joy or in struggle, disciples of Christ continue to trust his perspective and his power to carry us through life.

And with that trust in Jesus at the center of a believer's worldview and experience, she can move on to the second part of the Christian life.

Arrow 2: Honoring God

The fruit of a life given over to God is undeniable. When a person has a genuine attitude of repentance - trusting in Jesus' perspective on life and faith - the natural result is the fruit of repentance. That means you'll start actually living differently.[15]

---

15 http://www.pursuegod.org/how-to-live-out-a-pursuit-of-god/

Let's go back to the response of the first Jewish believers in the book of Acts. Pay particular attention to their words:

> ***Acts 2:37*** *Peter's words pierced their hearts, and they said to him and to the other apostles, "Brothers, what should we do?"*

Look at their reaction to the message of Jesus. "What shall we do?" A genuine encounter with the grace and forgiveness of Jesus causes us to act. The Christian life is not just a free pass to live however we want. We become a new people from the inside. And that means a change on the outside.

> ***2 Corinthians 5:17*** *This means that anyone who belongs to Christ has become a new person. The old life is gone; a new life has begun!*

This new life doesn't manifest itself immediately or perfectly, but it begins the moment a person comes to faith in Jesus. It grows from a new, deep desire to please God instead of pleasing ourselves. But how does it happen? How do we practically pull off this new kind of life? God does not leave it to us to become better people. Having been saved by grace - a pure gift from a generous God - we begin to live this new kind of life by grace. And God gives us three gifts to make honoring him a reality in our everyday lives.

The Spirit leads us. The Bible says that at the moment of faith God himself – by the Holy Spirit – takes up residence in our lives (Ephesians 1:13). This means that our new desire to honor God will be fulfilled not just by our own will power, but by God himself. This was God's plan all along for his chosen people, and he tipped his hand to his strategy centuries earlier through his prophet Ezekiel.

> ***Ezekiel 36:26*** *And I will give you a new heart, and I will put a new spirit in you. I will take out your stony, stubborn heart and*

> *give you a tender, responsive heart. And I will put my Spirit in you so that you will follow my decrees and be careful to obey my regulations.*

A Spirit-led life increasingly produces the fruit of the Spirit. God does not force these qualities on us, but they appear in our lives as a consequence of being connected to Jesus. Jesus told as much to his disciples:

> ***John 15:7-11*** *But if you remain in me and my words remain in you, you may ask for anything you want, and it will be granted! When you produce much fruit, you are my true disciples. This brings great glory to my Father. "I have loved you even as the Father has loved me. Remain in my love. When you obey my commandments, you remain in my love, just as I obey my Father's commandments and remain in his love. I have told you these things so that you will be filled with my joy. Yes, your joy will overflow!"*

Jesus made it clear: being a disciple will change the way you look. Connection to Jesus has a whole-life impact on the believer, and it's obvious to everyone looking on. Is this true of your life? Too many Christians in the church have no evidence of the fruit of a changed life. Jesus gave the first two - love and joy - in the passage above. Paul started with those items as he built his list in the letter to the Galatians.

> ***Galatians 5:22-24*** *But the Holy Spirit produces this kind of fruit in our lives: love, joy, peace, patience, kindness, goodness, faithfulness, gentleness, and self-control. There is no law against these things! Those who belong to Christ Jesus have nailed the passions and desires of their sinful nature to his cross and crucified them there.*

A disciple is someone who is committed to honoring God with his or her whole life, empowered by the Holy Spirit and changed from the inside out.

The Bible guides us. But the fruit of the Spirit is just the start. God's vision for us touches every part of our lives, and he has given us the Bible to help us get there. The Bible is God's very Word, handed down to us through the ages and kept pure by his own power. As Christians, we don't just follow our hearts to know what is right. We trust his Word and align ourselves with its perspective on the world.

> ***2 Timothy 3:16-17*** *All Scripture is inspired by God and is useful to teach us what is true and to make us realize what is wrong in our lives. It corrects us when we are wrong and teaches us to do what is right. God uses it to prepare and equip his people to do every good work.*

Allowing the Bible to be the ultimate authority for life and faith is an extension of the new attitude we have as Christians. We trust Jesus' perspective over our own opinions. And we find his perspective in the pages of scripture.

> *"So, how do we honor God?" Lexi asked. She and Sam had been Christians for all of a week, and they were still smiling.*
>
> *"Well, the Bible paints the picture," I said. We were having breakfast together, covering another topic from Faith 101.*
>
> *"I've never really read the Bible," Sam replied. "I know some stories here and there, but that's about it."*

"Yeah, that's fine," my wife Tracy replied. "As you read the Bible, you'll learn what God wants."

Sam looked a little weirded out.

"No, it's pretty normal stuff," I reassured him. "Everything you've seen in our life and relationships, that's what we're talking about."

"We love you guys," Lexi smiled. "We want to have a life like yours."

We wanted that for them, too.

"But is there anything we should be doing now to honor God?" She asked.

I was afraid of that question. I knew the answer, and Tracy and I had talked about it on the way to breakfast. We debated whether we should bring it up. After all, they were just a month away from their wedding date.

I couldn't resist.

"Well, there is one thing." I paused to take a breath. "It's about sex."

"I knew it!" Lexi hit Sam on the chest. "We're not supposed to have sex until we're married."

Lexi knew it from her Mormon upbringing, but she wasn't sure if it was a Christian value. Besides, most Mormons she knew didn't actually follow that particular rule.

"Sorry Sam," I replied. This was a whole new concept for him. "We weren't sure we should even bring it up. But as you read the Bible, it's pretty obvious. Sex is something God designed for marriage."

"Is God mad at us?" Lexi asked innocently.

"No, listen. We know you guys are already living together," Tracy explained. "That's pretty normal in our culture. We expected that you would be living like everyone else."

"Here's what we think you should do," I suggested in. "Make a commitment to purity for this last month. That's one of the simplest ways you can honor God right now. And it'll pay off in your marriage down the road. It'll prove that you are submitted to God's way, no matter what."

I glanced at Sam. I didn't want him to think he had just joined a cult.

"Be honest," I asked. "Can you handle it for a month?"

"Absolutely," he said. "If that's what God wants, we'll do it."

Other believers help us. The final great resource for the Christian life is other Christians. Faith is not a solo thing; we need each other. It's a team sport. That's why every Christian should connect regularly with a mentor or a small group. Paul explained why in his letter to the Galatians.

> ***Galatians 6:1-2*** *Dear brothers and sisters, if another believer is overcome by some sin, you who are godly should gently and*

> *humbly help that person back onto the right path. And be careful not to fall into the same temptation yourself. Share each other's burdens, and in this way obey the law of Christ.*

The law of Christ that Paul is referring to is probably the Greatest Commandment: love God, love people. That can't happen in isolation. We need each other to stay on the right path and honor God. This goes far beyond pointing out people's sin. The true essence of the law of love is that you don't want others to live on the path toward destruction.

This also means we should make a commitment to a local church. The author of Hebrews commanded it.

> ***Hebrews 10:24-25*** *Let us think of ways to motivate one another to acts of love and good works. And let us not neglect our meeting together, as some people do, but encourage one another....*

With the leadership of the Holy Spirit, the guidance of the Bible, and the help of mentors we can have victory in the second part of the Christian life, honoring God with our daily attitudes and actions.

Arrow 3: Helping Others Pursue God

Sadly, most Christians think that the Christian life has only two parts. They believe if they "pray the prayer" they'll get to heaven. The faithful ones go a step further, participating with God to live a new kind of life. But very few Christians feel the call of God on their lives to actively make disciples.

And that's the third arrow in a full circle Christian life. Once you've trusted Jesus for salvation, and as soon as you've begun to live a life that honors God, you're ready to help someone else pursue God through biblical mentoring (disciple-making).[16]

This, according to Jesus, is the only way to mature. Paul said it, too, back in Ephesians 4. When regular people are empowered to do real ministry, speaking the truth in love with the people around them in everyday relationships, something special happens. Those regular people end up deepening their own faith and growing more mature.

> ***Ephesians 4:15*** *Rather, speaking the truth in love, we are to grow up in every way into him who is the head, into Christ...*

Read it again. When regular people speak the truth in love, they grow up. They are no longer consumeristic in their faith, looking for someone else to feed them and make them strong. This was the secret of the early Christian church, the source of sustenance for the believers who had no Bible studies or mega churches or Christian concerts. They were disciple-makers, and carried along by a sense of mission and by the power of the Holy Spirit, they had what they needed.

> *"No, hold on, let me try to explain it again," I said, still standing at the whiteboard after almost an hour. We were all grad students in the mathematics department, but none of us understood the advanced matrix concepts we were studying.*
>
> *And the final was tomorrow.*
>
> *"It's all about understanding the kernel..." I was stalling for time. I didn't really understand what I was talking about, but neither did they. My style was to crunch the numbers until I got the right*

[16] http://www.pursuegod.org/how-to-grow-in-a-pursuit-of-god/

answers. But I didn't always understand the concepts at the deepest level.

It was frustrating.

"Here's what the prof has in his notes," I said, rifling through my papers one more time. I looked back at the board and continued trying to explain it.

Then it hit me. Suddenly, inexplicably, in a single instant of clarity, everything made sense. What I couldn't get in a semester of lectures and note-taking, I finally got standing at the whiteboard.

And what it took was being the teacher, not the student.

God created us, and he knows how we learn. Whether math or science or faith, we learn best when we are the teachers, not when we are the students. Even if we don't fully get it yet.

Imagine a church where every believer feels equipped to make disciples in a natural relational context. Neighbors reach out to friends and invite them to pursue the God of the Bible. Parents answer the call to be pastors at home, transferring their values to their kids through everyday conversations. And those same kids are eventually empowered to make disciples in their world, growing mature along the way as Paul said it would happen in his letter to the Ephesians.

> **Ephesians 4:13-14** *This will continue until we all come to such unity in our faith and knowledge of God's Son that we will be mature in the Lord, measuring up to the full and complete*

standard of Christ. Then we will no longer be immature like children. We won't be tossed and blown about by every wind of new teaching. We will not be influenced when people try to trick us with lies so clever they sound like the truth.

This is the church that Jesus envisioned, a church of full circle followers. They don't stop at trusting Jesus or even at honoring God. They go "all in" with their faith and help someone else pursue God.

"Bryan, I've got some great news." It was Lexi on the phone, with Sam listening in.

"What, tell me," I said expectantly.

"No, you've gotta guess first."

"You're pregnant!"

"Nope," she laughed. "Not that."

"You're ready to mentor someone?"

"Yes!" she shouted.

"Awesome!" I celebrated. "That's even better than the first thing."

"We thought you'd say that!" Lexi responded.

They had barely been Christians for a year, but they knew the goal. Since they put their faith in Christ, they had been praying for and expecting an opportunity to disciple somebody.

"We're not sure if we're ready," she confessed. "We don't feel like we know enough."

"C'mon, what's the third thing you learned in Faith 101?" I encouraged.

"We grow by helping someone else," she answered.

"That's right," I said. "If you wait 'til you're mature enough, you'll never mentor anyone." We had been over this. "Mentoring is the thing that will make you mature."

Think about how the world measures growth, maturity, or success. What's the "win" in the business world? It's about personal advancement. Greatness in our culture is a "me" thing. But not with Jesus.

> **Mark 9:33-35** *After they arrived at Capernaum and settled in a house, Jesus asked his disciples,"What were you discussing out on the road?" But they didn't answer, because they had been arguing about which of them was the greatest. He sat down, called the twelve disciples over to him, and said, "Whoever wants to be first must take last place and be the servant of everyone else."*

Jesus taught that we advance in the Kingdom of God by looking outward. It's the Kingdom upside-down of Jesus' world. Do you want to be great? Serve others. Do you want to reach the highest goal of the Christian life? Make a disciple. That's what Jesus did, and that's what he expects of his followers.

Full Circle in Matthew 28

Jesus envisioned a full circle approach to discipleship, and it can be seen clearly in the Great Commission.

> ***Matthew 28:18-20*** *Jesus came and told his disciples, "I have been given all authority in heaven and on earth. Therefore, go and make disciples of all nations, baptizing them in the name of the Father and the Son and the Holy Spirit. Teach these new disciples to obey all the commands I have given you. And be sure of this: I am with you always, even to the end of the age."*

Let's break down this passage to see the three arrows of a full circle Christian. Pull out a pencil and get ready to mark up the text.

First, underline the word "baptize". Many believers think "discipling" means to start Bible studies and help Christians grow in their doctrinal understanding. Think again! Why would that type of person need to be baptized?. The truth is, Jesus had in mind that his disciples would go out and engage people who didn't yet know about the kingdom of God. Those were the ones who needed to be discipled, not just the long time Christian in the pew next to you.

When Jesus talked about discipleship, the first thing he had in mind was what we would call evangelism. In the mind of Christ, discipleship and evangelism are not two separate programs in the church. Biblical discipleship, at least for the early disciples, started with evangelism. That's why the first step in our picture of discipleship is trusting Jesus. Coming to faith is the first part of a pursuit of God, hence the need for baptism.

Look back at the text. Jesus said to "teach these new disciples to obey all the commands I have given you". In today's church we might call this sanctification, and it's an important part of discipleship. A follower of Jesus doesn't just pray a prayer and then go on living in unrepentant sin. Something fundamental changes inside the heart of a new believer. He or she has become a new creation. And that leads to a radical change in everyday life.

The way we say this in our tools is that we live to honor God. The world has seen too many followers of Jesus who say one thing and do another. True biblical disciple-making includes walking alongside a follower of Jesus and helping that person live in a way that honors God. That's the essence of our second arrow.

Back to the text one more time. The very first word in the Great Commission is "go". Inherent in the call to follow Jesus is the call to go into the world and make disciples. When Jesus sent out his closest disciples 2,000 years ago, he didn't intend for them to be the only ones who would go out. This commission is for every follower of Jesus today. Jesus envisioned that his disciples would go make disciples. He did not mean for it to be a task only for professionals.

That's why the third arrow in our picture exists. Every believer is compelled to go, and to send out others who will go. Sharing the gospel without explaining the Great Commission is incomplete. Christians need to learn how to finish the job. When I lead someone to faith and to a God-honoring life, my job is only two-thirds complete. I need to teach him to go out and help the next person pursue God.

When we start helping someone else pursue God through disciple-making, we are pointing them to the same pathway that we are on. We are not walking out ahead, dragging them along. We are walking shoulder-to-shoulder, showing them how to trust Jesus and honor God just as we are doing ourselves. And when we help them make disciple-makers, this movement can go viral.

Ch 6. The PursueGOD Disciple-making System

Equipped with a clear definition of "disciple," we finally understood what the real win was at church. The goal was to make one more "full circle" follower of Jesus, which ultimately meant making one more disciple-maker.[17] But how? That would require a simple, measurable, reproducible process. And we had to build a tool.

"Pastor Steve taught us the secret."

Pastor Manny Carlos was pouring out his wisdom over lunch in metro Manila. I was hanging on every word.

"If you want to grow a church, preach a sermon," he continued. "But if you want to start a movement, write a curriculum."

I thought I heard him wrong. Everything else he had shared seemed so cutting edge and revolutionary. This seemed like something straight out of the 80's.

"What? Really?" I asked, shocked.

"That's right," he said. "Steve showed us how to make disciples by giving us booklets. Without it, we wouldn't know what to do."

"But with a curriculum, we exploded into a movement."

---

[17] http://www.pursuegod.org/what-mentors-make/

Those words rang in my ears for months after returning from the Philippines. I was resistant to a curriculum. If it wasn't old school, it was at least cult-like. Would Americans really go for that? Wouldn't it be too inflexible?

But we asked the pastors around the table. How did everyone make disciples in the past? The answers were all different. Some people used books. Others just used the Bible. Women liked DVD series and workbooks. Men liked something less formal. But we all held one thing in common: no one could really describe a reproducible method.

And that's why it wasn't happening. We didn't know what "it" was.

> *"I don't think you get it. I appreciate the effort, but we don't all have the gift." JD took another swing.*
>
> *We golfed 9 holes together every Monday morning, and I was using it as an opportunity to disciple him. But this was years ago, before mentoring was a thing at our church.*
>
> *"It's not about a gift," I replied. "It's a calling on the life of every follower of Jesus. We're all supposed to make disciples."*
>
> *JD was a retired Air Force fighter pilot, a godly and humble Christian. But he wasn't confident that he had anything to say to anyone. And besides, now he was a commercial pilot and didn't exactly have an opportunity to share his faith.*
>
> *"Suppose I find someone willing to listen," he finally said. "What do I even say to him?"*

"Just do with him what I've been doing with you," I answered.

He thought for a minute.

"And what, exactly, have you been doing with me?" He asked.

Now I had to think for a minute.

"Reading the Bible, explaining theology..." I trailed off. The truth was, I hadn't given much thought to the process.

He finished making his point. "When you figure it out, let me know."

So we had to figure it out. How could we build a curriculum easy enough for the average American to use? What would it look like? Could it work for both men and women? What about families and students? How would this curriculum be distributed? And how could it stay flexible enough to meet the needs of an ever-changing culture?

We wanted to create an "easy button" for disciple-making, but we didn't have the budget to print workbooks or produce DVDs. It had to be simpler, more scalable. And the more we drilled down, the clearer it became to us. We had to find a way to help people talk about stuff that really mattered to them.

Our tool had to empower conversations.[18]

---

[18] http://www.pursuegod.org/about/

Philip's Conversation

The story of Philip and the Ethiopian eunuch provided a great visual for what we were trying to accomplish. Seeing the eunuch in his chariot, Philip took the opportunity to engage in conversation.

> ***Acts 8:30-35*** *Philip ran over and heard the man reading from the prophet Isaiah. Philip asked, "Do you understand what you are reading?" The man replied, "How can I, unless someone instructs me?" And he urged Philip to come up into the carriage and sit with him. The passage of Scripture he had been reading was this:*
>
> > *"He was led like a sheep to the slaughter.*
> > *And as a lamb is silent before the shearers,*
> > *he did not open his mouth.*
> > *He was humiliated and received no justice.*
> > *Who can speak of his descendants?*
> > *For his life was taken from the earth."*
>
> *The eunuch asked Philip, "Tell me, was the prophet talking about himself or someone else?" So beginning with this same Scripture, Philip told him the Good News about Jesus.*

Notice Philip's simple strategy. He was attentive to what God was doing in the eunuch's life, and he engaged him in a conversation. He pointed the conversation back to Jesus and shared the good news with him. God was already doing a work in the seeker's heart; Philip was simply there with confidence and a readiness to share.

And there's something else we noticed in Acts 8. The "Philip" in the story is not Philip the Apostle, the man called by Jesus to be one of his 12 disciples. Philip from Acts 8 is a different guy, a regular follower of Jesus who was chosen in Acts 7 to meet the practical needs of the church and serve alongside Stephen. In other words,

Philip was not a pastor, he was a regular person in the church. And his going out and sharing Jesus with the Ethiopian eunuch is a practical illustration of the Ephesians 4 principle.

Pastors equip regular people. Regular people make disciples.

But how did it happen? We saw it in verse 35: "Philip opened his mouth...."

Biblical mentoring, we decided, boiled down to one thing: a meaningful conversation. If Philip hadn't opened his mouth, the eunuch wouldn't have heard about Jesus. Mentoring was all about sharing the right truth at the right time in the context of a real relationship.

It's what Paul described it in Ephesians.

> ***Ephesians 4:15*** *Instead, we will speak the truth in love, growing in every way more and more like Christ, who is the head of his body, the church.*

We identified the key phrase: *truth in love*, a biblical worldview communicated through a real relationship. And this also made clear to us what the holdup was. We knew that most people already had real relationships. It was *sharing the truth* that was difficult for most of them. If we could empower our people to have intentional, Christ-centered conversations with people in their world, we could help them become disciple-makers.

Building the Library

Here was our job, as far as we could tell: equip regular people for Christ-centered conversations. Somehow, in our increasingly shallow internet culture, we had to empower followers of Jesus to make disciples through real life, actual conversations.

But most Christians didn't feel equipped for these conversations. "What if they stump me with a question? What if I'm not an expert in an area? Why can't I just bring them to a pastor to be discipled?" We knew we had to build something that could alleviate these real concerns.

We decided to build an online library of conversations that covered a wide variety of topics. The idea was to equip a believer and a non-believer alike to have equal access to content that articulated a biblical worldview. The believer could use the library to prepare for mentoring and to strengthen his or her knowledge base. The non-believer (or new believer) could use it to seek answers to spiritual questions on just about any topic. When both people came together to talk, God would show up for the conversation too.

We began building our online library at pursueGOD.org with a commitment to a few core values:

> **Use short videos.** We knew that if regular people, especially guys, were going to use the curriculum, the core content couldn't be more than about 5 minutes in length. The same held true for young people. If we really wanted it to be useful, we'd have to keep it short.
>
> **Include discussion questions.** The whole goal, after all, was to empower conversations. We had to include a few great questions in the curriculum to help spark those conversations. Writing good questions is difficult. As our team got bigger, we got better at it.

Platform regular people. Celebrity preachers can be great, but building a library only on their content would send the wrong message. YouTube was already platforming secular ideas from regular people; we knew we could do the same thing with the Christian worldview. The more "regular" people we had doing it, the more acceptable the message would be in a postmodern world.

Keep it "simple biblical". So much content out there made sense only to a veteran Christian. Other curriculum was so focused on a particular theological perspective that we thought it got too deep into the "weeds" for the average Christian. "Simple biblical" to us meant that it was accessible to just about anyone, and it didn't make people feel like idiots for not being a Calvinist or a dispensational premillennialist.

Make it free. Christian curriculum is a multi-million dollar industry. We thought it was weird to charge money for God's truth when secular ideology is free just about everywhere else. If this thing was going to reach people who didn't know Jesus, we couldn't start charging for it.

As we started to use the online tools as a baseline resource for our disciple-making, we began to see the effect that Paul described in Ephesians 4.

Ephesians 4:15-16 *Instead, we will speak the truth in love, growing in every way more and more like Christ, who is the head of his body, the church. He makes the whole body fit together perfectly. As each part does its own special work, it helps the other parts grow, so that the whole body is healthy and growing and full of love.*

Using tools that empowered conversations - rather than using a curriculum that encouraged our people to be Christian consumers - began to grow everyone up. Regular Christians were able to *articulate and absorb* the truth of God's Word, rather than to just listen to it. Slowly, mentoring started happening within the church walls. Christians who wanted to give it a try got connected to new believers who needed some help. And everyone started growing.

How It Works

Over time, we had built a massive library of conversation-starters, and people started using it. We knew that the goal was to create more "full circle" followers of Jesus, but we were still missing a fundamental element. What were the steps that disciple-makers had to take in order to walk with someone from beginning to end until they went "full circle"? We discovered that there were three main "phases" in disciple-making: Invite, Invest, and Empower.[19] We added them to our image:

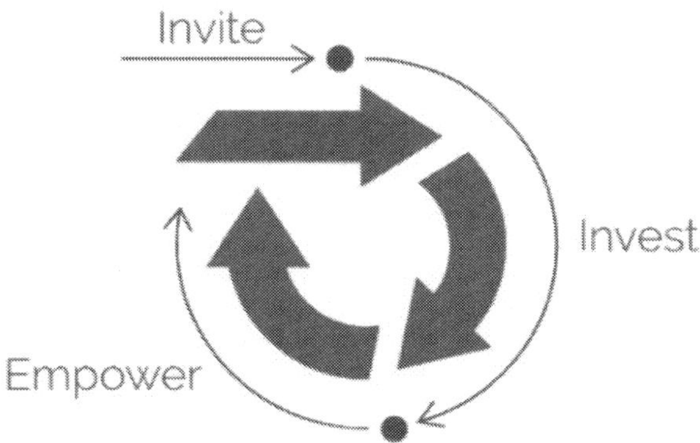

[19] http://www.pursuegod.org/how-to-make-disciples/

The first phase is the "invite": simply invite someone to talk about a topic that matters to them. Whether marriage, money, dating, parenting, self-worth, theology, or any number of subtopics, the key is to offer up valuable information that makes a practical impact on another person's life. Everyone is looking for answers, and most people don't know where to find them. A good friend is the person who can point the way.

"Hey Jason, do you mind if I send you a video link on marriage?" Ryan asked his friend at work. "It's just a short video, but I think it might really help."

Ryan was a friend from church that I was mentoring. When I challenged him to mentor someone from work, his coworker was the first name to come to mind.

Jason had already been talking to him about marriage troubles.

"That would be great," Jason responded. He was desperate for some help, and he trusted Ryan's advice.

Five minutes later Jason was at Ryan's door.

"Can we talk about this now?" Jason had already watched the video, and he was ready.

"Of course, come on in." Ryan closed the door behind Jason and they started digging in to the discussion questions.

An hour later they were done. It was a powerful conversation.

"Thanks Ryan, that was really helpful," Jason shared. "Can we do another one next week?" He had noticed that the marriage section of the library was filled with additional topics.

"No problem. Which one do you want to do?" asked Ryan.

"Can we just do all of them, one week at a time?"

A mentoring relationship was born.

Now the invite isn't a sales pitch. It's not about knocking on doors and handing out tracks. That kind of invite doesn't work for most people today, and few Christians would feel comfortable doing it in the first place. Our approach is more relational. In my life, I usually extend the invite by sending a link to one of our topics via text. I prayerfully pick a topic that matters to another person, and then I send it with a low-pressure invitation to talk about it over coffee or on the phone. I'll follow up every week or two with additional topics, laying the groundwork for a future mentoring relationship.

The texting method is just one option.[20] In my church I can be more direct, leveraging my pastoral status to invite people into a mentoring relationship with myself or someone else.[21] In my home I can be even more direct, discipling my kids with our tools and getting to the topics they need the most.[22]

Making an invitation starts with a certain amount of boldness. That's what the disciples prayed for in the early church, and we still need to pray for boldness today.

---

[20] http://www.pursuegod.org/3-ways-to-invite-into-a-discipleship-relationship
[21] https://www.pursuegodnetwork.org/making-the-handoff
[22] http://www.pursuegod.org/how-mentoring-works-in-the-parenting-years

Acts 4:29 *And now, O Lord, hear their threats, and give us, your servants, great boldness in preaching your word.*

For me, being invitational has become a lifestyle. It was awkward at first, but knowing what I was inviting people to - intentional, meaningful, value-added conversations - made all the difference. Now my invitations are natural and relational, not heavy-handed or pushy. I'm confident that others will benefit from the conversations we'll have together, and the online tools make it easy for me to move to the second phase.

The investing phase is where real disciple-making happens. This is where you cover topics on a weekly or monthly basis, talking face-to-face or over the phone. It's the "easy button" for on-demand disciple-making. It employs the "FLEX" conversational method:

1. **Find a topic.** You've already sent a few topics, and those are a great place to start. But there are literally thousands of additional topics to choose from on our websites. Use pursueGOD.org for standard discipleship topics, pursueGODkids.org for kid-friendly topics, pursueGODnetwork.org for pastors and church leaders, and FLEXTALK.org for those who aren't quite ready for spiritual conversations. Find a topic (or series) that fits your need, and send it out ahead of time.
2. **Learn about it.** When you send out your topic a few days early, you're giving the other person an opportunity to take ownership for what they're learning. Encourage them to dig in to the topic, clicking on related links and looking over the discussion questions. And be sure to do the same thing yourself in preparation for the conversation. This step gives the Holy Spirit room to start working on your hearts even before you sit down to talk.

3. **Explore it together.** When it's time for the conversation, use the questions provided and mix in some of your own queries to make it more personal. Ask good questions and learn to listen to others and to God. If you get stumped, just admit it. If the conversation goes sideways, consider covering a related topic in your next meeting.

Continue to cover topics with the "full circle" goal in mind. In the investing phase, you're helping people with the first two arrows: trusting Jesus (faith) and honoring God (life). Don't rush the process, and prayerfully choose the topics that will get you there.[23]

"Are there any conversations in the library about God?" Jason asked. He had been covering marriage topics with Ryan for 4 months, and he was ready to explore something else.

"Uh, yeah," replied Ryan, taken off guard. He viewed the resources as God-centered already, but Jason must have seen it more as a marriage thing.

"I think I'd like to talk about Christianity," offered Jason. He was Mormon, but he knew Ryan was different. He had some lingering doubts about his faith, and he trusted Ryan to lead him along the way.

They started in on some fundamental faith topics. Just a few weeks later Ryan helped Jason to trust Jesus for salvation.

A disciple was born.

---

[23] http://www.pursuegod.org/the-3-phases-of-pg-mentoring/

The PG discipleship system is easy and free, but what makes the system so powerful is its reproducibility. That's what the third phase of disciple-making is all about.[24]

Once you've invited and invested, then you're ready to empower people to go do what you've been doing. That means taking them through the training process online[25] and following up with them until they're making disciples, too. You've already modeled the method and the tools, and now it's their turn to go out and make disciples.

This is what Jesus had in mind: disciples who would make disciples who would make disciples, until everyone had the opportunity to pursue God through a meaningful relationship with another pursuer of God. It's exactly what Paul was trying to get across to Timothy.

> ***2 Timothy 2:2*** *You have heard me teach things that have been confirmed by many reliable witnesses. Now teach these truths to other trustworthy people who will be able to pass them on to others.*

Paul wanted Christians to help someone else *who could help someone else* pursue God. That makes us more than disciple-makers. Technically, we're disciplemaker-makers. Jesus wants this thing to go beyond the first generation to the second generation and beyond. He wants us to use a viral strategy in making disciples. But it only works if everyone has permission to empower another disciplemaker-maker.

I've tried to make disciples my whole life, but until I used a system with simple tools and a clear outcome, I could never replicate my

---

24 http://www.pursuegod.org/close-the-loop/
25 http://www.pursuegod.org/train

efforts through another person. My impact would almost always stop with the person I was mentoring, because I wasn't doing it in a fundamentally reproducible way. I was always investing, but I never finished the job. Now I empower the people I'm discipling, and my impact is already starting to have an exponential effect.

Let's look at the image one more time:

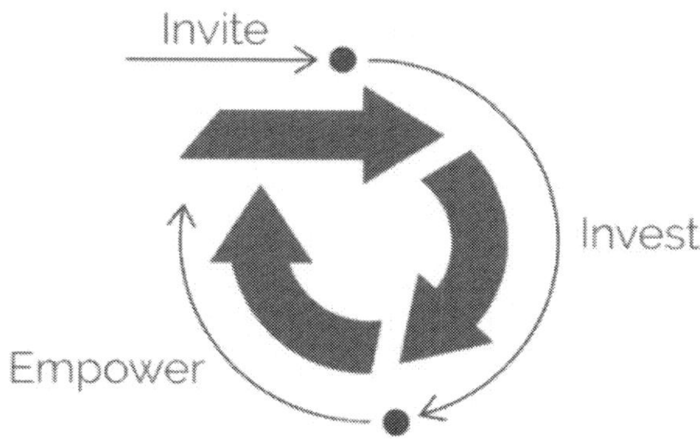

The goal isn't to get someone through a curriculum, but to help them around the circle. That means helping them trust Jesus, honor God, and eventually make disciples.

Are you ready to re-discover the movement that Jesus envisioned all along? Invite, invest, and empower - and together we'll change the world.

To join the movement, visit www.pursueGOD.org/join.

Epilogue

"So are you concerned about Pastor Steve leaving?" I asked my friends at Victory Church. Steve Murrell was their apostle, their beloved pastor and the architect of their discipleship culture. He had come 25 years earlier for a short-term missions trip. Their ministry exploded and he never left. He calls himself an "accidental" missionary. Now he was heading back to Nashville, committed to splitting time between the two locations.

"Not at all. Why would we be concerned?" They responded.

"Many churches would implode after losing their main guy. Are you sure that's not going to happen?" I wanted to see how confident they were in their system.

They didn't bat an eye.

"One time Steve showed up at a newer campus of Victory. He was standing outside with the crowd the whole time, and no one even recognized him," they shared. "It's not about Pastor Steve. We're not worried."

It was true. As I walked through their corporate offices, I couldn't even find a picture of their planting pastor. They spoke so highly of him as a staff, but there was no sense that he was the main guy. It had been that way for 25 years.

"You'll see when Pastor Steve transitions back to the US," they explained. "We'll keep growing, we're sure of it. Pastor Steve showed us how to make disciple-makers. We doubled in the last five years with him. We'll double again in the next five without him."

I was inspired by their optimism, but secretly I doubted it. Going from 17,000 to 35,000 is impressive enough, but doubling again once you've hit those kinds of numbers - that seemed unthinkable.

Five years later we visited the church again. Our jaws dropped when we heard the numbers.

70,000. And counting.

Made in the USA
San Bernardino, CA
02 September 2019